MY EYES CLOSED

A CHAPBOOK ON IDENTITY, GRIEF, AND HOPE

WENDELYN VEGA

Copyright © 2021 by Wendelyn Vega

All rights reserved.

No part of this book may be reproduced in any form or by any electronic or mechanical means, including information storage and retrieval systems, without written permission from the author, except for the use of brief quotations in a book review.

For permission requests, contact:

info@wendelynvega.com

Visit the author's website at WendelynVega.com.

ISBN: 978-1-7347796-1-5

Cover Photo by **Lisa Fotios** from **Pexels**

Cover Design by Wendelyn Vega

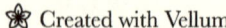 Created with Vellum

For those who mourn

1. DESCORT

> I wonder what it's like to be so sure.
> To look at the world without question
> And think
> "I am the master of my own mind and spirit.
> Who can challenge me?"

2. VOICES

Voices,
Sounding a dissonant chord.
Noises,
Drumming the ears of the horde.
All of the messages
Sounding out loud;
How to listen to
So overwhelming a crowd?
All have a voice,
That much is clear.
But if everyone's speaking,
Who's going to hear?

3. **I AM...**

> I am Unheard
> I am a voice that cries alone
> in a dark and icy void.
> I am Unknown
> I am a tear that falls unseen
> to a barren desert's sand.
> I am Unloved
> I am a flower that wilts and fades
> in the shadow of empty dreams.

4. CASCADE

What I want to say
Is trapped within roiling emotions.
The words I'm so close to elude me.

Heartburn and heartache catch
In my throat, keeping me from
What I want to say.

My hands shake, and the floodgates
Won't open. The key
Is trapped within roiling emotions.

The words, my fair-weather,
pretty, posing friends,
the words I'm so close to elude me.

5. HEARD

Though my lips move
There is no voice.
There's silence here,
But not by choice,
Though ears are closed
And hearts are locked,
I will press on
Though I am blocked.
At my sorrow
You stand and jeer.
Cold countenances
'Round me leer.
This silent frame
Must stand and fight
As icy wind
Attacks my light.
Though thunder blocks
My every word,
My only wish
Is to be heard.

6. BLOOD BLACK

Blood black against the sterling tile.
Another line in the little book.
Blood black behind a lying smile.
Another line in the little book.
Blood black against the sticky ground.
Another line in the little book.
Blood black behind a secret found.
Another line in the little book.
Blood black beneath the scorching sun.
Another line in the little book.
Blood black before a smoking gun.
Another line in the little book.
Blood black against the driven snow.
Another line in the little book.
But no one really wants to know.
Another line in the little book.

7. HEARTSICK

I choke down bile
at the back of my teeth.
How much blood is enough?
You suffocate me
with your ransom of hate,
and you ask me why
I can't breathe.
When will you keep
the promise you made?
Or were those all lies
as well?
What you have done
is a murder of faith,
a gun at the back
of my trust.
Where didn't you learn
trust is not only earned,
it is beating, breathing,
Alive?
I choke down blood

from the wound in my heart.
Whose last words are enough?

8. TOKEN

If you were looking, you'd see
my trembling hands, my mute plea.
You don't really care for me
As long as I keep you free.
Firm like the root of a tree,
My branches a sad decree.
I cannot stay your token.
A broken cadence are we.

9. ACROSTIC

My crime is this: I am
Your greatest mythic fear.

For you, I am
A mass encased, a memorial
To hate and despise.

Be that as it may, I am
Loath to let you
Assess and assign
Creation's place for
Kindred like me.

Because I am not
Open for your
Discussion, nor am I
Yours to name.

10. GRIEF

> The crack of a broken heart
> Rends silent the art-worn knell
> The song of the church can't reach
> The story each vein can tell

11. CURTAINS

And the rest of us?
Well,
we mean well.
We tread softly.
Too softly,
not softly enough.
We get angry.
Too angry,
not angry enough.
But when
we've talked too long
to see the danger
too close to our eyes,
Who will fight
for
the rest of us?
Well,
we mean well.

12. CINQUAIN

Really?
You haven't been
trying all this time to
defend yourself from an honest
mirror?

13. OLD FRIEND

Who do you think you're kidding
With your glittering veneer
Dazzling everyone
Who should know better?
I've seen you
At your ugliest,
Showing your truest soul
To the people who need you
Most.
I've seen you dragging
Your treasures through the mud,
Chasing after
The next worst thing.
You don't fool me.
I still see you.

14. 6

> When clouds hang over,
> It is normal to worry,
> More so if they're dark.

15. 4

When rain falls heavy,
It is normal to sorrow,
More so if you're soaked.

16. THIS IS QUITE TERRIBLE…

My eyes are quite heavy
And well prone to hurt
My limbs are in water
My soul is on earth

The truth is a bevy
Of feathers and dirt
Settled on my shoulders
The price of the birth

Of a haphazard glory
From unending thought
And fingertip panic
To challenge my worth

There's an art to levy
A nightmare curt.

17. THE BOP

    Blooming backward isn't all that difficult
    No one has to teach you how to watch
    a dream shrivel and die under the scorching
        heat
    of a desert sun or the poisonous torrent of a
        monsoon
    rain. It comes naturally to all of us, our
        daily habit, a
    pastime we acquire.

    The flower is heartier than you think it is.

    Why not just lay your head down and
        close your
    eyes while the hope of the future passes
        you by?
    Turn your thoughts to the past and
        wonder what
    might have been if you had been better
        sooner,

If you had opened your eyes. But you won't
 open your
eyes. It's too late now. The rain is already
 falling. Half
your crop is destroyed. There's no time to
 protect
the other half while you wish you had more
 time.

The flower is heartier than you think it is.

If you open your eyes, the dream might be
 dead.
It might be too late. It might be too
 long. You
might find that the rain and the wind
 and the
sun have left you far from the place where
 you started
and far from the place you must go. But
 then,
you might not. What then?

The flower is heartier than you think it is.

18. SWALLOW ME WHOLE

Dark of the night,
You desire me to bow.
Want me under your yoke,
Want me pulling your plow.
You want me broken,
You think you know how
To rule in my heart,
But I promise you now:
Dark of the night,
You will not win my soul.
You won't crush me or break me
You won't gain control.
I will fight back,
I will not duck or roll.
If you want to take me,
Swallow me whole.

19. A LETTER

>
> Please don't be disappointed;
> I know this has caused some pain:
> Your dreams and life disjointed,
> Your prayers still a sad refrain.
>
> It must be so confusing
> As things seem to all go wrong.
> This verse is not your choosing,
> But the life is still your song.

20. SURRENDER

Rage, oh rage
the voices say.
They call in
grating tones
the weary souls to battle
once more.
Will they be silent
if we lay down our weapons
and surrender
for the last time?

ALSO BY WENDELYN VEGA

My Head Bowed: A Chapbook on Depression, Anxiety, and Faith

Kulebra

Wendelyn Vega is a poet, fantasy author, and international woman of timidity. When she's not writing, she enjoys reading, trying out new recipes, and playing with the two mini tigers she keeps in her house.

www.ingramcontent.com/pod-product-compliance
Lightning Source LLC
Chambersburg PA
CBHW060346080526
44583CB00014B/1079